FOREIGN LANGUAGE EDUCATION
THE EASY WAY

With best wishes!
S. Krashen.

Also by Stephen Krashen:

Under Attack: The Case Against Bilingual Education
Language Education Associates

The Case for Late Intervention
(with Jeff McQuillan)
Language Education Associates

*Every Person a Reader: An Alternative to the California
Task Force Report on Reading*
Language Education Associates

The Power of Reading
Libraries Unlimited

The Natural Approach
(with Tracy Terrell)
Prentice Hall International

Fundamentals of Language Education
Laredo Publishing

All of the above titles are available from:

Language Education Associates
Post Office Box 3141
Culver City, CA 90231-3141 USA

www.LanguageBooks.com
input@LanguageBooks.com

Toll free (US & Canada): 1-800-200-8008

Tel: +1 (310) 568-9338 • Fax: +1 (310) 568-9040

FOREIGN LANGUAGE EDUCATION
THE EASY WAY

Stephen D. Krashen

1997
Language Education Associates
Culver City, California

FOREIGN LANGUAGE EDUCATION THE EASY WAY

Language Education Associates
Post Office Box 3141
Culver City, California 90231-3141 USA

(800) 200-8008 • fax: +1 (310) 568-9040

http://www.LanguageBooks.com

e-mail: input@LanguageBooks.com

In Latin America contact:
Fenix Language Institute
Apartado Postal 102-B
Cuernavaca, Morelos
Mexico

Tel/fax: (73) 11-48-99 • e-mail: fenixmex@mail.giga.com

Publisher's Cataloging-in-Publication
(Provided by Quality Books, Inc.)

Krashen, Stephen D.
    Foreign language education the easy way / Stephen D. Krashen. —
1st ed.
    p. cm.
    Includes bibliographical references.
    Preassigned LCCN: 97-74416
    ISBN: 0-9652808-3-7

    1. Language and languages—Study and teaching.   I. Title.

P51.K73 1997   418'.0071
                                QBI97-40991

Contents

Introduction

In this monograph, I outline how a foreign language teaching program can help students acquire conversational language, and then move, in as painless a way as possible, to "academic" language, the latter term covering the use of language in areas such as school, business, politics and science. It attempts to overcome a problem all foreign language programs have: how to help students progress to advanced levels in the absence of native speakers.

In part one, we briefly review some language acquisition theory. In part two, the foreign language program is outlined, and in part three we discuss some current issues in foreign language education, including ways in which FL (foreign language) differs from SL (second language); while there are differences, I will argue that an approach based on comprehensible input is valid and appropriate for FL programs. In fact, more application of comprehensible-input based methodology will help solve some of the problems that FL students face. We also discuss the "problem" of teachers who do not speak the target language as a native language as well as the issue of whether we must use only "authentic" texts.

Some Theory

Current language acquisition theory claims that we acquire language in only one way, when we understand messages, that is, when we obtain "comprehensible input". Thus, we acquire when we understand what people tell us or what we read, when we are absorbed in the message. More precisely, we acquire when we understand messages containing aspects of language that we are developmentally ready to acquire but have not yet acquired.

It has also been argued that certain affective factors are conducive to language acquisition: acquisition proceeds best when the acquirer's level of anxiety is low and self-confidence is high, that is, when the acquirer's "affective filter" is down. Smith (1988) hypothesizes that for literacy development, the child needs to consider himself or herself to be a potential reader and writer, a potential member of the "literacy club". Similarly, it can be hypothesized that language acquisition proceeds better when acquirers consider themselves to be potential members of a group that uses the language. (Note that I wrote "a group" and not "the group". I will return to this point later.) When we join a club, or at least feel that we are welcome to join, the affective filter goes down and we acquire those aspects of language that mark us as members of the group that uses that language.

Comprehensible input (or "CI") results in language acquisition, subconscious tacit competence. Conscious language learning ("knowing about" language) is limited in function: it can only be used as an editor or Monitor. After we form our sentence mentally, we can apply consciously learned rules before we speak in order to improve our accuracy. But the Monitor can only be successfully used when stringent conditions are met: The language user must know the rule, must be focused on form, and must have time to apply the rule. For most people, these conditions are only met on grammar tests, and in editing writing.

Some people are able to use some grammar rules while conversing. These are people who know the particular rules very well and can occasionally manage the conversation in a way that gives them time to use the rule. This is a very difficult trick, and is also risky: some people plan their next sentence while the other person is talking, which results in a perfect sentence that has nothing to do with what the other person said.

Occasional monitoring "on-line" appears to be easier when the performer has acquired a great deal of the language, but even then only a small part of grammatical knowledge can be utilized.

Consciously learned grammar is, in a sense, "heavy"; the brain can carry and use it only with great difficulty. Acquisition, on the other hand, is "light"; it is easy to carry. Someone who has acquired a great deal of a language can use their acquired competence to "support" some learning. But it takes a great amount of acquisition to support even a small amount of conscious learning.

Error correction is aimed at conscious learning, not acquisition: Correction is supposed to help students arrive at the correct version of the conscious rule. Research shows, however, that error correction often has no effect. When an effect is present, it is modest, and it occurs just when the Monitor hypothesis predicts it: when the performer knows the rule, has time to apply it, and is concerned about correctness (Krashen, 1982).

The reading hypothesis is a special case of the comprehensible input hypothesis, it claims that reading for meaning, especially free voluntary reading, is comprehensible input, and is the source of much of our competence in literacy, our reading ability, writing style, much of our vocabulary and spelling competence, and our ability to use and understand complex grammatical constructions.

An aspect of the input hypothesis that is extremely important in discussing its' application is that given enough comprehensible input, structures students are "ready" to acquire are invariably present in the input. We do not have to make sure that certain structures or vocabulary are covered. If students get enough comprehensible input, they will be.

The evidence for comprehensible input has been presented in detail elsewhere (see e.g. Krashen, 1982, 1985, 1994a). Briefly, the more comprehensible input people obtain in the target language, the more acquisition takes place. This appears to be the case for both the informal environment (outside of school) as well as the formal environment (classroom), and for both language and literacy development.

Note that the actual relationship between the amount of CI obtained and individual progress depends on whether the CI contains aspects of the target language that the acquirer has not yet acquired, but is developmentally ready to acquire. Thus, progress for very advanced acquirers may be slow, even if they live in the country where the language is spoken, because the comprehensible input they receive has little in it that they have not already acquired.

Rival Hypotheses

In addition, there is good evidence that "rival hypotheses", other hypotheses concerning the development of language and literacy, are not correct. The "instruction hypothesis" claims that we acquire by first learning rules and vocabulary items consciously, and then "practicing" them until they become "automatic". There are several reasons to doubt that the instruction hypothesis is correct. First, the system of grammar, vocabulary, etc. that needs to be acquired is too complex to be learned consciously. Second, there are many cases of people who have developed high levels of proficiency in both second language and literacy without instruction. Third, studies show that the effect of grammar teaching is very limited. Gains after direct teaching are short-term, and appear only on tests in which students are focused on form (Krashen, 1992, 1993a).

A second rival hypothesis is the output hypothesis, which claims that we acquire language by producing it. There are several versions of the output hypothesis, but they all suffer from these problems: First, output is too scarce to make any important impact on language development; language students speak relatively infrequently in language classes, and people write much less than they read. As Smith (1988) has pointed out, we don't write nearly enough to account for the acquisition of complex systems such as spelling and the other conventions of writing. Second, studies also show that increasing student writing does not increase writing ability (Krashen, 1994). Output can help indirectly, however. Writing has important cognitive benefits—it can be of great help in problem-solving. Spoken output can contribute to language acquisition indirectly by encouraging input via conversation. Both writing and speaking, I suspect, also help the acquirer feel more like a member of the "club", the group that uses the target language.

Components of a Foreign Language Program

Orientation

The first component of a FL program should be an orientation, a brief introduction to language acquisition theory. It is important to tell students something about the philosophy underlying our approach for two reasons: First, because the approach outlined here is radically different from traditional approaches, we need to justify our pedagogy to students and in some cases to their parents. Second, our goal is not simply to bring students to a certain level in the foreign language. Our goal is to give them the tools to continue to improve on their own, to make them "autonomous". Knowing how language is acquired will help ensure that this will occur.

Orientation can be done in the primary language at the beginning level, and covered later, in more detail, as sheltered subject matter teaching at intermediate levels, as will be discussed below.

Beginners

Beginning level methods based on comprehensible input include Natural Approach (Krashen and Terrell, 1983) and Total Physical Response (Asher, 1994). What these methods have in common is that they attempt to fill the classroom hour with aural comprehensible input. The use of physical movement (Total Physical Response), pictures, and realia helps make second language input comprehensible. In this section, I focus on Natural Approach.

In Natural Approach, students are not required to respond in the second language in the beginning stages, but if they do, errors are not corrected and students are not required to respond in full sentences. This procedure is based on the input hypothesis and findings showing that error correction has little or no effect. Allowing the student to respond in the first language, a practice borrowed from Canadian immersion programs, facilitates communication.

Thus, in Natural Approach, speech is allowed to "emerge". According to language acquisition theory, speech is a *result* of acquisition, not its cause. In Natural Approach classes, there is no pressure on students to use language in production beyond their capacity. Students are never forbidden from speaking, however.

Pre-Speech Stage

In early stages, no student response is required at all. During this stage, which Terrell called the "pre-speech" stage, physical movements are used (TPR), as well as activities that combine TPR with pictures. The teacher, for example, can give out pictures and then ask:

> "Who has the picture with the boat? (Student raises hand and shows the picture.) Right, John has the picture with the boat. Who has the picture with the trees? Right. Mary has the picture with the trees."

Other techniques require only minimal student response, such as single words or phrases. For example, in the following activity, students need only respond with a name:

Instructor: Who has red hair?
Students (any or all can answer): John
Instructor: Who has long hair?
Students: Mary, Susan ...

Early Production

In the "early production" stage, students respond with single words or short phrases. Terrell provides the following example of interaction at this stage aided by a picture:

"Is there a woman in this picture? (yes) Is there a man in the picture? (no). Is the woman old or young? (young). Yes, she's young, but very ugly (Class responds no, pretty). That's right, she's not ugly, she's pretty..." (From Krashen and Terrell, 1983, p. 79).

Speech Emergence

In the "speech emergence" stage, students produce longer, more complex utterances. It must be emphasized that during this stage, students will make many grammatical errors. These errors will gradually disappear not by more careful monitoring of output or correction but with more comprehensible input.

Of course, Natural Approach does not insist that the stages be strictly adhered to: students in "speech emergence" can certainly engage in activities that require no response. But students are not forced to produce responses beyond their stage of development.

In all Natural Approach activities, students are never called on individually. Rather, Natural Approach uses what Terrell has called "random volunteered responses", in which anyone in the class can respond without raising their hand, and several students can respond at the same time. Random volunteered responses are not as orderly as responses in traditional classrooms, but are closer to real communication, and appear to reduce student anxieties considerably.

Syllabi

Comprehensible input-based methods are organized—they have syllabi and lesson plans, but they are not organized according to a grammatical syllabus. Rather, the syllabus is based on activities that students will find interesting and comprehensible. Thus, details of what is included will vary according to the age, interests and backgrounds of the students. All students, I predict, will like listening to the teacher read aloud from interesting, comprehensible texts, and will like hearing stories.

Variation in syllabi is possible because of the hypothesis, mentioned earlier, that given enough comprehensible input, all aspects of grammar that the student is ready for will be present in the input. The teacher's responsibility is to present messages that are interesting and comprehensible, and the acquisition of grammar, it is predicted, will take care of itself.

Direct Teaching of Grammar

There are two justifications for including the study of grammar, but there is no justification for making it the main part of a language teaching program or for teaching it to children.

One justification is for Monitor use. While the Monitor is very limited, it is of some value. The

Monitor can be used in the editing phase of composing, and can help the writer increase accuracy for those aspects of grammar and punctuation that are late-acquired (and that for some people are never acquired). There is substantial variation among adults in knowledge of and interest in grammar, but most writers can consciously learn the more straight-forward rules.

It is not necessary to memorize these rules. All that is necessary is that students learn to use a grammar handbook. Of course, to use a grammar handbook, one has to understand a fair amount about grammar as well as some traditional terminology—when the handbook advises the student that "whom" is used as a direct object or object of a preposition, one has to know what these things are. Thus, while memorization is not necessary, understanding is.

A second justification for grammar study is as linguistics: Some students are interested in the structure of language as an object of study, and are fascinated by language change and dialects. This material can be included at the intermediate level as sheltered subject matter, to be discussed below. This kind of detail is, however, not necessary or even particularly helpful for using a second language and students in such classes need to know they are studying linguistics, not acquiring the language.

While there is a place for grammar study, it must be emphasized that it is peripheral. The core of the program should be acquisition via comprehensible input. There is, in my view, no reason to include grammar study in programs for children. The ability to understand any but the simplest grammatical rules occurs when children attain the stage Piaget calls "formal operations". Attempting to teach grammar to young children is simply not worth the effort. It can be done much more easily when they are older, during the teen-age years. (It is interesting that the capacity to learn formal grammar increases at about the same time as the capacity to do abstract mathematics: We begin the study of algebra in the early teens.)

Dr. Kato Lomb, quite possibly the most accomplished polyglot in the world, is deeply interested in grammar, and includes grammar study as part of her personal program in working on new languages. In her view, however, grammar is not the most important aspect of developing competence in languages; grammar study should be optional for adults, and consist only of presentation of the most straight-forward rules. Requiring children to study grammar is, in her opinion, "absurd" (Krashen and Kiss, 1996).

The Research

Comprehensible-input based language teaching methods have done very well in the language acquisition research: Students in comprehensible input-based classes typically outperform traditional students on all measures involving communication (reading comprehension, conversation), and do as well, or slightly better, on form-based tests (see e.g. Asher's studies, summarized in Asher, 1994; Hammond, 1989; Nicola, 1989; Swaffer and Woodruff, 1982; Wolfe and Jones, 1982, Nikolov, 1995).

Negative Reactions to the Natural Approach

There have been two kinds of complaints about Natural Approach and related methodologies. One is the observation that Natural Approach students produce speech that is highly inaccurate: they make lots of mistakes. Terrell (personal communication) has explained what is going on in this situation. Terrell notes that it is true that in comparison to classes taught with traditional methods, Natural Approach students appear to make more mistakes. The reason for this, however, is that Natural Approach students can speak much more fluently than traditional students can; thus, teachers hear more errors! Evidence that this interpretation is correct is the finding that Natural Approach students are just as accurate or are more accurate than traditional students on form-based tests.

Another complaint has been made by some foreign language teachers who note that students who enroll in higher-level classes after comprehensible input methodology in lower level classes are not up to the standards of previous years' students. Sternfeld (personal communication) investigated these charges at one university and found that they were, in fact, true. There was, however, a very good reason for these "declining standards". Many more students were continuing on to higher levels. In previous years, most of the students who took higher level courses were those who had had considerable exposure to the language outside of the classroom, who spoke it at home or who had lived in the country where the language was spoken. A Natural Approach student will, of course, be no match for a native speaker or someone with extensive real-world experience with the second language. Cononelos (1988; cited in Sternfeld, 1992) confirmed that this was the case: Of 109 students who took traditional lower level German classes, only four went on the higher levels. In comparison, nine of 22 students in a comprehensible-input based methodology class went on to advanced German. While the latter group made up only 17% of all fifth-quarter students surveyed, they accounted for 69% of the students in these classes.

Some New Developments:
Narrow Listening and Handcrafted Books

In narrow listening, described in detail in Krashen (1996), acquirers collect brief tape-recordings of proficient speakers discussing a topic selected by the acquirer. Acquirers then listen to the tape as many times as they like, at their leisure. Repeated listening, interest in the topic, and familiar context help make the input comprehensible. Topics are gradually changed, which allows the acquirer to expand his or her competence comfortably. Narrow listening is a low-tech, inexpensive way to obtain comprehensible input, and is also an easy way to get to know speakers of other languages.

Dupuy and McQuillan (in press) describe an innovative and simple way of providing interesting and comprehensible reading material for beginning foreign language students. Handcrafted Books are texts written by intermediate students to be read by beginning foreign language students. The stories can be original or retellings, and are written without the aid of a dictionary, to insure comprehensibility. (Dupuy and McQuillan note that if intermediate students do not know a word, the chances are that beginning students will not know it either.) Authors are also invited to illustrate their books, and the text is corrected by the instructor. Completed volumes are placed in a library so they can be accessed easily. Dupuy and McQuillan reported that intermediate students found the experience of writing Handcrafted Books to be useful, enjoyable, and satisfying. Handcrafted books also go a long way toward satisfying a serious gap in materials.

Intermediates

Clear evidence that something is very wrong with current programs in North American universities is the fact that very few students in advanced foreign language classes at the university level get all their preparation from language classes. Graman (1987) reported that only eight out of 85 students in advanced undergraduate Spanish reported no Spanish outside the classroom. As noted just above, Dupuy and Krashen (in press) studied five intermediate foreign language classes and reported that only about 10% of the students had not used the language outside the class ,or were not native speakers. In both studies, it was found that those with more outside experience reported more comfort in class, and Dupuy and Krashen reported that their "false intermediates" got better grades as well. The kind of intermediate level suggested here will result in much better prepared students in advanced classes, and make it possible to actually "come up through the ranks" in foreign language education.

I recommend two overlapping components for intermediates. Our goal at this level is to bring students to the point where they can continue to improve on their own. This means that they will be able to converse comfortably with native speakers as well as read authentic texts without extensive use of a dictionary. Note that this does not mean that their speech or writing will be error-free. No language teaching program has ever achieved this, nor is it a reasonable goal. If we bring students to the stage where they will be able to improve on their own, and have the knowledge of how to improve more, their accuracy and fluency will continue to increase. This goal is ambitious enough, and very few language programs have achieved it.

(For those who think such a goal is a lowering of standards, it is, in my view, an ordinary view of education we all accept: One does not expect a recent graduate to be a master. Rather, school is supposed to give one enough competence to begin to practice one's profession, and professional experience promotes continuing development and learning.)

The intermediate level is also intended to be a bridge between "conversational" language and "academic" language (Cummins, 1991), the latter term covering the language of school, business, science, politics, philosophy, etc.

Component 1: Sheltered Popular Literature

Sheltered subject matter teaching is subject matter teaching made comprehensible for the intermediate student. Sheltered subject matter teaching has two important characteristics:

(1) It is for intermediates only, not for beginning students and not for advanced students or native

speakers. Sheltered teaching is not comprehensible for beginners - these students need methods such as TPR and Natural Approach, described earlier. When advanced students or native speakers attend sheltered classes, they make life difficult for intermediates, by pulling the input level too high. When all students are more or less in the same linguistic boat, it is easier to make the input comprehensible.

(2) Sheltered subject matter classes are subject matter classes: They are not language classes. If there are tests or projects, the focus is on the subject matter, not the language. This focus, paradoxically, insures more language acquisition: If we test grammar and vocabulary, students will study grammar and vocabulary. This is not effective. But if we test subject matter, or require projects based on subject matter, students will come to class, do the reading, engage in discussion, and, thereby, obtain more comprehensible input. The result will be more language acquisition, and thus, more grammatical accuracy and larger vocabulary. Research on sheltered subject matter teaching, summarized in Krashen (1991), shows that students in these classes acquire at least as much of the second language as students in regular second language classes, and usually more. In addition, they learn impressive amounts of subject matter. Thus, students in these classes get both language and subject matter at the same time, and the language acquired is academic language.

Sheltered subject matter teaching has been used successfully in several areas. For FL, a very logical place to begin is sheltered popular literature. The goal of such a class, or module, is to introduce the student to a wide range of texts in the second language in order to help the student establish a reading habit. In addition, sheltered popular literature can give the student insights into the culture of speakers of the foreign language.

Here is a possible syllabus for English as a foreign language:

(1) <u>The comic book.</u> Comic books contain a substantial amount of language, about 2000 words. Readability levels of comics range from about grade two (e.g. Archie) to grades 6 or higher (superhero comic books), which means they can be read by students at different levels. Comics such as Archie solve a big problem for our students: Reading material that is comprehensible but also interesting. Archie deals with teenagers and it is written at the second grade level (I thank Deborah Krashen for pointing this out to me). Several second language acquirers, as well as first language acquirers, have reported that comics, for them, were the conduit to harder reading (e.g. Mathabane, discussed in Krashen, 1993).

(2) <u>The magazine.</u> Nearly everyone finds at least some magazines to be very interesting.The language is often exactly at the right level for less

mature readers. Rucker (1982) reported that providing free magazine subscriptions for junior high school students in the United States resulted in superior gains in standardized reading test scores.

(3) The newspaper. Newspapers vary in difficulty level, as well as complexity of information, which is very good news for teachers and students. USA Today, for example, is very readable, and can provide the competence necessary to read more demanding newspapers.

(4) Novels. The teen romance, the Harlequin, best-selling love stories, and classical romances provide a natural sequence that present a view of men and women that should lead to interesting discussion. Similarly, the cowboy story of the 1940's and 1950's, the detective novel of the 60's and 70's, and the more recently popular spy novel provide a characterization of masculine behavior that deserves examination. Science-fiction novels come in adolescent versions, and include the popular Star Trek series, enough reading to keep the most devoted Trekkie busy for a long time.

In selecting what students will read, I think that teachers should consider their own interests as well. The teachers' enthusiasm (or extreme distaste) for a book will add a charge to the teaching, and make it much more interesting. The goal is to find texts that are interesting for both students and teachers.

To keep interest alive, some teachers select different texts every year. What is crucial, in my view, is that teachers be allowed, and encouraged, to select the particular texts they want to teach. The Ministry of Education might suggest that certain categories be covered, and even have a list of recommended texts to help teachers who are not familiar with all the available literature, but the text selected must be the teacher's choice. When we teach popular literature, we are not dealing with a canon; rather we are trying to introduce students to a wide variety of possibilities in the hope that they will find what they are interested in and establish a reading habit.

My suggestion is that sheltered popular literature classes be taught as literature: All students will read the same texts, or groups of students will read the same text (and discuss them in "literature circles"; see below) and the texts will be discussed for their "message" as well as for the insight they give as to the characteristics and values of the culture that produced them.

[Consider, for example, Archie. Why does Archie prefer Veronica to Betty? (They are identical twins except for hair color.) The answer, I think, is that Veronica has more self-esteem. What does Jughead represent? Is he a representative of counter-culture or a "nerd"? What is the function of Pop's Soda Fountain? Does it represent neutral turf or society's meeting place, such as the bar on the T.V. show, "Cheers"? Is Riverdale High School the typical North American high school? What values are encouraged by parents, teachers and teenagers in Archie? And of course, the most profound question one can ask about Archie: When will he graduate from high school? Unlike Beverly Hills 90210, Archie and his friends never move on. Archie, Betty, Veronica, Reggie and Jughead have been students at Riverdale High School since 1941 and have experienced the longest incarceration in the history of education!]

The text for such a class will not be the usual reading comprehension text, with short, difficult paragraphs and comprehension questions. It will be, rather, the literature itself, e.g. a package of selected comic books, including one child's comic, one Archie, a few superhero comic books, leading up to a comic novel (DC's Watchmen and Batman Returns are well-written, provocative classics); a Louis L'Amour Western, a Sweet Valley novel, or perhaps one from Sweet Valley Kids (written at the second grade level), Sweet Valley Twins (written at the grade four level), and one from Sweet Valley High, the original series written at the grade five or six level. Some classes might enjoy a book from the Nancy Drew series.

In order to teach such a class, the teacher, of course, must be an expert on popular literature. This is not difficult to do, and many teachers already have a good knowledge of the field. Our job is to remain current, and bring in the latest books and magazines when they are relevant. Teachers should also be adept at reading aloud to students; even older students can get "hooked on books" when they hear part of the story read to them (see e.g. Trelease, 1995).

Component 2: Free Voluntary Reading

Free reading is a powerful means of developing academic language. As noted above, the goal of the popular literature class is to help students establish a free reading habit. Free reading can be integrated into the program in two ways:

(1) As Sustained Silent Reading (SSR): In SSR, students simply read for pleasure for a short time each day, from five to 15 minutes. There is no accountability, no book reports, no requirement that readers finish the book they start. According to the research, students who do SSR typically gain at least as much on standardized tests as students who participate in traditional programs, and usually do much better if the program lasts long enough (Krashen, 1993). SSR is ideal for the intermediate level but can also begin earlier.

(2) A more intensive version of SSR, one that can follow the semester or module of sheltered popular literature, is individualized reading, in which the entire class period is devoted to self-selected

reading (Appleby and Conners, 1965). In individualized reading, students are encouraged to read deeply in the area or areas they are interested in. When students finish their book or magazine, or decide to drop it, a brief conference with the teacher is held, to review progress and to discuss what the student will read next.

Extensive Reading in Japan

Beniko Mason's studies show that individualized reading (which she terms "extensive reading") works very well in English as a foreign language, and also confirm the value of using pedagogical texts (Mason and Krashen, 1997). Mason's students were university level EFL students in Japan, taking a required English class. In each study, students in "extensive reading" classes read graded readers, both in class and as homework. There was some "accountability" in these classes (which is not the case in Sustained Silent Reading programs in the United States), but it was minimal: students had to write short synopses and keep a diary in Japanese, recording their feelings, opinions, and progress. Students in comparison classes followed the traditional grammar and translation-based curriculum.

In Mason's first study, experimental students were in a special class for students who had failed EFL (termed a Sai Rishu, or retakers' class). Students were pre and post tested with a cloze test, which required them to fill in missing words in an English text. As presented in table 1, the extensive readers made larger gains than, and nearly caught up to the traditional students, who began the semester far ahead.

Table 1
Pre and Post Test Scores

	PRE TEST		POST TEST		GAIN	
	mean	sd	mean	sd	Mean	sd
Extensive reading	22.55	11.54	31.40	11.43	8.90	6.22
Traditional	29.70	8.23	33.05	8.24	4.35	6.47

test: 100 item cloze test

sd: standard deviation

from: Mason and Krashen (1997)

Perhaps the most important and impressive finding of this study is the clear improvement in attitude shown by the students who did extensive reading. Many of the once reluctant students of EFL became eager readers. Several wrote in their diaries that they were amazed at their improvement. Their diaries also indicated that they understood the stories. Also of interest is Mason's observation that students did not progress linearly from easy to hard books. Some students read easy books after reading some more difficult texts, and then returned later to harder books.

In subsequent studies, Mason showed that extensive reading was superior to traditional instruction in programs lasting for a full academic year for both university and community college students. She also demonstrated that extensive readers improve in writing as well as reading (Mason and Krashen, 1997).

Reactions to Light Reading

Several studies done in the United States confirm that foreign language students enjoy extensive reading. McQuillan (1994) surveyed a university level ESL class and a university level intermediate Spanish class. Students in both classes participated in ten weeks of extensive reading of popular literature, including newspapers, magazines, short stories, graded readers, and novels (the latter for ESL only). Most reading was assigned, but some was self-selected. At the end of the ten weeks, attitudes were probed. Students in both classes felt that reading was more beneficial and more pleasant than grammar study (table 2; results for both classes were very similar and are combined in the following table).

McQuillan notes that his positive results may be due to the fact that his subjects had just experienced the light reading program. Students who have not had this experience might not be aware of how pleasant and beneficial reading is.

	READING	GRAMMAR INSTRUCTION
Most beneficial	78% (38)	22% (11)
Most pleasant	84% (41)	16% (8)

Table 2.
Students' Reactions to Reading and Grammar Instruction

(assigned and self-selected reading combined)

from: McQuillan (1994)

Dupuy [forthcoming (a)] presents additional confirmation in a French as a foreign language setting. Nearly all of her 32 students (86%) reported that they had done no pleasure reading in French at the start of the fourth semester class. The focus of the class was free reading; as in Mason's studies in Japan, accountability was minimal; students only had to record what they read and were invited to give their reactions. 88% of the students (28) felt that the reading had helped to develop their general competence in French, with the most impact felt in vocabulary and reading comprehension. 82% (40) said they were more likely to read on their own in French after the class, and 94% said they would recommend the class to others.

In Dupuy [forthcoming (b)], fourth semester university French students participated in a slightly different form of self-selected reading. Small groups of students selected the same book and then met in "literature circles" to discuss what they had read. 97% of the class felt that the literature circles made reading more pleasant and contributed to their reading comprehension ability. All students felt that hearing others' views of the reading helped them understand the texts better.

Narrow Reading

Both SSR and individualized reading encourage narrow reading, staying with one author, topic or genre: there is no attempt to cover different text types or time periods. Research strongly suggests that voluntary narrow reading is more effective than the broad, survey-type reading that is assigned by teachers: readers typically select a wider range of reading as they progress (LaBrant, 1938); the books children select on their own are typically more difficult than those assigned by teachers: free reading is not always easy reading (Southgate, Arnold, and Johnson, 1981; Bader, Beatch, and Eldridge, 1987). In addition, while discourse types do vary, there is a fair amount of overlap between different styles. Thus, anyone who reads deeply in any area will acquire a substantial amount of the academic style. A student of EFL who has read 50 Agatha Christie novels or 50 Barbara Cartland romances will have a much easier time with a New York Times editorial than an EFL student who has not done the same amount of pleasure reading.

Sticking to the same kind of text, reading the work of a single author, or reading books in a series, provides the reader with a familiar context and thus helps ensure comprehension. In support of this claim, it has been found that better readers tend to read more series books (Lamme, 1976). Also consistent with this view are recent reports of impressive progress in English as a second language by female adult acquirers who read extensively from the Sweet Valley High series, a series written for girls (Cho and Krashen, 1994, 1995a, 1995b).

The Sweet Valley Studies

Cho's subjects were women in their 30's who, despite years of formal EFL study in Korea and considerable residence in the United States, had made little progress in English.

Cho first suggested that her subjects read books from the Sweet Valley High series, adolescent fiction written for girls ages 12 and older. These books proved to be too difficult; they could only be read with great effort, and with extensive recourse to the dictionary. Cho then tried Sweet Valley Twins with her subjects, a set of novels based on the same characters at a younger age, written for readers ages 8 to 12. Once again, however, the texts were too difficult. Cho then tried Sweet Valley Kids, novels dealing with the same characters at an even younger age, written for readers ages 5 to 8. Her subjects, all adults, became enthusiastic Sweet Valley Kids readers.

Cho reported significant vocabulary growth in her readers (Cho and Krashen, 1994), and gathered informal evidence of their progress, including reports from their friends (Cho and Krashen, 1995a). Perhaps the most impressive result is the report of one of the subjects one year after she started reading Sweet Valley books. After one year, this subject, who had never read for pleasure in English prior to this study, had read all 34 Sweet Valley Kids books, had read many books from the Sweet Valley Twins and Sweet Valley High series, and had started to read Danielle Steele and other authors of romances in English.

Of course, the Sweet Valley series is not for everyone, but it should not be difficult to find appropriate texts for those with other interests, as well as similar readings in other languages.

For these programs to work, two conditions must be met: first, as noted earlier, teachers must know a great deal about popular literature, including adolescent literature. Second, books must be available, a point we will return to later.

A New Definition of "Authenticity"

Mason and McQuillan's success with pedagogical readers (see also Hafiz and Tudor,

1989) forces us to reexamine the issue of "authenticity". The usual definition of "authentic" is "a text written by native speakers for native speakers". Perhaps a better definition is this one: "A text that is interesting and comprehensible". In my view, it is the second definition that is appropriate for language education. In other words, there is nothing wrong with reading texts that are specially prepared for second and foreign language students, as long as they are interesting and comprehensible. They can be a helpful first step, leading to the reading of texts that are authentic in the traditional sense. Insisting that all reading be from texts written by and for native speakers usually results in a great deal of incomprehensible input and frustration.

Even though some pedagogical texts are written with heavy constraints, with a focus on particular structures and vocabulary, some are, nevertheless, good reading and a student who reads a variety of such texts will make progress.

A Three-Stage Plan

The following plan makes explicit what has been implicit in the discussion so far, and is, in my view, a kinder, gentler way. I predict that it will develop competence much faster than previous approaches. It provides interesting, comprehensible input at all times.

Stage I: Reading artificially constructed texts, which will bring students to a level of competence high enough so that easy authentic texts (light reading) are comprehensible.

Stage II: Reading "light" authentic texts, which will bring students to a level of competence high enough to understand at least some "academic" or "serious" texts.

Stage III: Reading authentic, difficult texts.

Within each stage, students are encouraged to read "narrowly," choosing texts they find interesting and gradually expanding their reading as they follow their interests. Narrow reading, as noted earlier, helps ensure comprehensibility.

Note that providing comprehensible texts at every stage eliminates the need for extensive teaching of strategies for dealing with difficult texts. Instead, it allows them to emerge, the same way very competant readers naturally develop the ability to deal with difficult texts.

As Victoria Rodrigo has pointed out to me, when readers can select their own reading, there will be some overlap among the stages. A student may read an easy stage II novel and then may choose a stage I artificially constructed text, letting interest guide the choice. This is exactly what Beniko Mason's students did.

Developing Academic Language

Someone who has done a great deal of light reading will find academic texts much more comprehensible than someone who has not. Nevertheless, light reading alone will not insure the acquisition of academic language. There are ways of taking some students a bit farther, into academic language itself. This can be done in two ways:

Narrow Academic Reading

Applying the same principles to the acquisition of "academic competence" means setting up a program that is much simpler than the traditional approach: It entails narrow reading in the students' area of interest. Students of politics could read newspapers, news magazines, and political journals. Students of science could read Science News, OMNI, Scientific American, and scientific journals, specializing in their area of interest. Those interested in business will read Forbes, the Wall Street Journal, the Economist, and Fortune.

Students will be able to progress rapidly in their reading development because of interest in what they are reading as well as having background knowledge. They will, in addition, acquire a great deal of academic language in general, because there is considerable overlap among styles—no matter what academic style readers select, for example, they will acquire a great deal of sub-technical vocabulary common to all fields, and the style they become familiar with will probably be used in neighboring fields.

Such a program can be set up in-class, similar to individualized reading described above, as a tutorial, and / or as part of sheltered subject matter instruction when enough students are interested in the same topic. Of course, a problem with the latter solution is that few foreign language teachers are prepared to teach sheltered classes in specialized areas. There are two areas, however, in which many language teachers are fully qualified: Literature (this time with a large "L") and Language.

Sheltered Subject Matter Teaching:
Literature and Language

Once students have read a great deal of popular literature, they will be ready for heavier material. In my opinion, such a class should be optional; students will have done a considerable amount of Literature study in their own language, and will have learned some of the lessons this study has to offer.

A sheltered subject matter class in Language may be attractive to a large percentage of students. As mentioned above, some students may be interested in the study of the structure of the second language, its' history and its' varieties. As an optional class, sheltered Linguistics could delve into universal grammar, how and why language changes, register, and the issue of "correctness" in language. In addition, this class can supplement the orientation given at the beginning and give students much more detail, this time in the target language, on how language is acquired and how literacy is developed.

Notice that components 2 (Sheltered Subject Matter Teaching) and 3 (Free Voluntary Reading) can overlap. For example, we can continue sustained silent reading while students are doing sheltered classes, and in some institutions students may be able to do one or more sheltered classes in Literature and Language while they are engaged in narrow reading in a topic of interest. In fact, the combination of aspects of components 2 and 3 could serve as standard preparation for the university foreign language major.

Issues in Foreign Language Education

FL Versus SL

The ways in which the foreign language (FL) classroom situation is thought to differ from the second language (SL) situation include the following:

(1) Students in the FL situation lack opportunities for using the language outside the classroom, because native speakers are not available.

(2) Teachers in FL classes are often not native speakers of the target language. Thus, FL students may be exposed to imperfect models.

(3) FL students do not have a "club" to join because they are not seeking to become part of another culture.

(4) In many FL situations, there is little time for FL instruction.

Concern 1: The Lack of Native Speakers Outside the Classroom

At the beginning level, FL and SL speakers are in exactly the same situation: they are dependent on the classroom for comprehensible input. For FL students, there is no comprehensible input outside the classroom. For SL students, the input outside the classroom is not comprehensible. For this reason, language classes are extremely valuable for the SL student: They give the acquirer the comprehensible input that the outside world will not provide or will, at best, provide reluctantly.

The best methodology for beginning SL should also thus be the best methodology for beginning FL. In fact, most of the research supporting the superiority of comprehensible input-based methods has been done in the FL, not the SL context (see references listed above).

The SL student clearly has an advantage at the intermediate level. This advantage applies mainly to conversational language. SL students can continue to develop their conversational language competence as soon as they are competent enough to understand some of the input they hear outside of class. This does not, however, insure the acquisition of academic language.

Approaches used for the development of academic language utilized in second language situations can also be used in the FL situation: sheltered subject matter teaching and light pleasure reading. Much of the research supporting sheltered subject matter teaching, in fact, has been done in foreign language contexts, including French as a foreign language in USA (Lafayette and Buscaglia, 1985) and Canada (Edwards, Krashen, Wesche,

Clement, and Krudinier, 1985), and EFL in Hong
Kong (Ho, 1982). Evidence showing the
effectiveness of in-school free reading also includes
studies done in the FL situation, involving EFL in
the Fiji Islands (Elley and Mangubhai, 1983),
Pakistan (Hafiz and Tudor, 1989), Singapore (Elley,
1991), and Japan (Mason and Krashen, 1997).

Free reading is not only an important bridge to
the acquisition of more complex language; it also
allows the FL student to maintain contact with the
target language, and to continue to improve, despite
the absence of native speakers.

Kato Lomb

A spectacular case of using free reading in this
way is Dr. Kato Lomb, whom we met above in the
discussion of grammar. Dr. Lomb has lived in
Budapest her entire life, and yet has acquired 17
languages. Her experience is thus very relevant to
foreign language education. Her primary method
of acquisition, and means of staying in touch with
her languages, is reading. When possible, she
utilizes aural input, from conversation, radio, and
on the job as an interpreter. It has often been very
difficult to get this kind of input. When she began
Russian, for example, it was during the Nazi
occupation of Hungary, and use of Russian was
forbidden. In addition, books were not plentiful.
She thus evolved an alternative, her "core novel"
method.

She selected one novel in the target language and read it very thoroughly, preferring novels to language textbooks because of the artificial language used in the latter. Often, it was a difficult novel (the first English author she read was Galsworthy), but when easier reading was available, she took advantage of it. When she started working on Russian, she tried some "serious" novels but found them difficult. Then she and her husband moved into an apartment that had been previously occupied by a Russian family that had to leave hastily and she discovered that a number of Russian romance novels had been left behind. She read them eagerly: "Without hesitation, I started reading them ... I worked so hard to understand them that even today I remember some passages" (Lomb, 1970, p.12, passage translated by N. Kiss). Because of the romance novels, her Russian improved, and by 1943, she read Gogol while in bomb shelters. She occasionally rereads the "core novel" years later, in order to bring back her knowledge of the language.

She says she does nearly all her pleasure reading in other languages. Of course, Dr. Lomb is aware that reading alone will not suffice to fully understand the oral, everyday language. She notes that "Those who use my method may find difficulty in the oral language" (p.87).

Dr. Lomb is clearly a reading enthusiast: "A book can be put in our pocket, it can be thrown away, we can write in it, we can tear it, lose it and buy it again ... we can read during breakfast, after we wake up, and [unlike working with a private teacher] we don't have to phone it when we don't have time ... we may be bored with it, but it is never bored with us" (p. 83).

Developing Conversational Ability
Without Native Speakers

The FL student will never have all the advantages of the SL student in acquiring more advanced conversational proficiency, but the current situation can be improved.

First, free voluntary reading can make some contributions to conversational ability. Many novels contain a substantial amount of conversational language. Cho's subjects, in fact, reported that everyday language was much more comprehensible to them after reading the Sweet Valley series.

A second approach, also low-tech, is the use of audio and video-tapes, including films, TV, and radio programs. If FL students have access to a wide variety of aural comprehensible input in this form, it will make a great contribution to the development of conversational ability. FL students should be able to select listening material according to their interest and level. Someone interested in science-fiction, for example, should have access to tapes of Star Trek TV shows, novels, and films. Someone interested in mysteries should have access to TV programs such as Columbo, Murder She Wrote, and Hitchcok films. Of course, in order for this to be possible, a very wide selection is necessary, with respect to both subject matter and difficulty level.

Written and aural input work well together. A student who has read a few Star Trek novels will have an easier time understanding the TV shows and vice-versa.

The Library

What all this leads to is the establishment of a library of print and aural comprehensible input. To my knowledge, this has never been attempted. I have seen several libraries for foreign language students; they typically contain a small collection of books, mostly classics. What I have in mind is a vast collection of light as well as "serious" reading—comic books, magazines, novels, etc., and light as well as serious viewing and listening - quiz shows, comedy, drama, documentaries, etc. to provide the comprehensible input missing from the FL students' environment. Such a collection would allow the foreign language student to read and listen for pleasure for several hours per day.

There are no serious obstacles to establishing such a library in many institutions. The materials are relatively inexpensive: Videos of films have never been less expensive, and comics, magazines, and paperbacks are affordable. Note that many foreign language programs are quite willing to spend huge sums of money on hi-tech equipment that lacks both theoretical and practical justification. For the price of one computer, consider how many paperback novels one could buy for a foreign language library.

At the moment, many teachers are taking up the slack and purchasing books with their own money for students' reading, while the school system purchases texts that are not used, or used resentfully. This is unacceptable. When interesting reading is not supplied by the Ministry of Education, and teachers must buy it themselves, teachers are in an impossible ethical dilemma: if they do not buy books, the students will have nothing to read. If they do, and the students read them and progress, the textbook gets the credit and the error is perpetuated. It is as if the teachers were sending their own money directly to the textbook publishers.

Because self-selection of reading and listening guarantees comprehension and interest, students need not be tested on what they read: there need be no "accountability", no comprehension questions or quizzes. This is highly desirable, as it is likely that testing will detract from the pleasure of reading and listening.

Some students may not take advantage of the library, however. It could be argued that accountability is necessary to insure that all students do the reading and listening. The answer to this objection is that the reading and listening material should be so interesting that students will want to read and listen. In most cases of reluctant readers I am familiar with, there was a lack of interesting reading material available. It is quite true that we can "lead a horse to water but we cannot make him drink", but first we must make sure that the water is there.

Concern 2:
When Teachers are not Native Speakers

When teachers are not native speakers, there is the concern that students will be exposed to imperfect models of the target language. One aspect is the fear that teachers will not be able to provide the quality and quantity of input needed for language acquisition.

To answer this, we first need to repeat that the FL class is not intended to bring students to the most advanced level in language development. The goal is to develop intermediates, to bring students to the point where they can use the language outside the classroom. Even with this more modest goal, it remains the case that some FL teachers do not have the competence to help students attain it. The answer, in my view, is not to hire native speakers with no knowledge of pedagogy. There are things that can be done.

First, we can supplement the aural input in the classroom with reading and listening material, as described earlier. The teacher's responsibility is to help the students develop efficient reading strategies, or, rather, to facilitate their emergence. As noted earlier, this is best done by engaging students in extensive reading.

A few strategies can be taught directly. I suspect those that can be taught are those that help students overcome bad instruction. Here is one example: Even students who are excellent readers in their first language sometimes adopt inefficient strategies when reading in their second language. The most common is the tendency to look up every unknown word. Pointing out that this practice is not necessary, that we acquire vocabulary far more efficiently and quickly through understanding the message (reading for meaning) and building up knowledge of the meanings of words gradually (Nagy, Herman and Anderson, 1985), will encourage students to skip words they don't know in their pleasure reading, and to select texts in which the number of unknown words is not overwhelming, which will free them from the burden of constantly referring to the dictionary. Similarly, students can be advised not to be concerned about understanding every word while listening. This kind of advice can be given in the students' first language.

Another valuable teaching function that could be done in the first language is to give students background knowledge on what is available for reading and listening in the target language, as a supplement or substitute for sheltered popular literature, discussed earlier. This function provides an additional benefit: as the teacher gets familiar with the contents of the library and keeps up with current reading and listening options, his or her competence in the target language will continue to develop.

Concern 3: Accent and "Joining the Club"

If the teacher is not a native speaker, students will, it is feared, acquire the teacher's imperfect accent. This concern is only a problem if the only input students get is from the teacher, or from other students who speak with a similar accent. If other sources of input are available, such as the aural input that is part of the library described above, the problem will be reduced.

In addition, it appears to be the case that we do not necessarily get our accents from the input we hear the most; we get our accents from the group we identify with, usually our peers (Beebe, 1985). In Smith's terms (Smith, 1988), we talk like members of the club we want to join, and are invited to join. The same is probably true of foreign language students: students are unlikely to want to talk like their teachers.

The preference for peers over teachers is reviewed in Beebe (1985). (Beebe also cites less common cases in which teachers are preferred over peers as models, demonstrating that it is group membership that is the key factor.) Nikolov (1995) presents an excellent example of peer over teacher preference in the FL situation: Her students of EFL in Hungary "accepted and copied the teacher up to the age of 10-11" (p. 173). But at around this age, the children turned to their peers as models: When fellow students returned from an extended stay abroad at about age 10 or 11, their newly acquired authentic accent was not approved of by the others. But when a boy returned from England after a month after grade 7, the other children adopted his informal style. Interestingly, the boys maintained aspects of the informal style, preferring "yeah" to "yes" while the girls did not, eventually returning to "yes".

If club membership determines accent, the question then is what club foreign language students should join. Some second language acquirers have an obvious club to join: citizens of the country they have immigrated to. Need FL students develop loyalty to another country to get a good accent? The answer, in my view, is "no". There are clubs other than national groups to join. (This is why I noted earlier that acquirers need to join "a group", rather than "the group".) In the case of English as a foreign language, one can, for example, join the club of international business people or scholars. Members of this club often speak English quite well, with very good accents.

Concern 4: The Time Problem

A common complaint in the FL situation is that time is limited. In FL teaching, a student may be exposed to the target language for only a few sessions per week. There are several responses to this concern.

First, beginning second language students have exactly the same problem, because input in the informal environment is not comprehensible for students at this level; thus, their only source of comprehensible input is the classroom.

Second, just because time is restricted does not mean we should return to traditional, form-focussed methodology: comprehensible input-based methodology is faster. As noted earlier, students in comprehensible input-based classes consistently outperform traditionally taught students on communicative tests and do as well or better on form-focussed tests.

Third, even a few sessions a week, over a few years, will do the job. Recall that the goal of the language class is not to develop perfect speakers of the language, but to develop intermediates, students who can continue to improve on their own (e.g. by using the library described earlier). This goal is attainable after a reasonable time. Just how long depends on several factors, including the L1-L2 relationship (when the target language is more closely related to the first language, acquisition is faster because cognate vocabulary makes input more comprehensible) and the age of the student.

Conclusion

Foreign language students do not have the advantages that second language students have, but there are many ways of improving the situation. The crucial element is the free reading/free listening library, which can supplement classroom comprehensible input and help non-native speaking teachers continue to develop their own competence in the target language.

With this conception, the role of the foreign language teacher changes, but in a direction that will, I predict, make life easier and more interesting. Currently, beginning foreign language classes are form-based. After one to two years, the program is typically devoted to reading the classics. Both of these approaches are frustrating. Few beginning foreign language students have an appreciation for grammar, and few intermediates are interested in, or prepared for classical literature.

With the modifications proposed here, beginning language teaching will be based on comprehensible input, which will be less frustrating for students and teachers; less grammar will be taught (with none taught at all to children) which will be much easier for students to handle. Instead of requiring students to think about grammar all the time, they will only be asked to do it when it does not interfere with communication, as in editing, and they will only need to learn (but not memorize) the more straight-forward rules of the language consciously (Krashen, 1982). My prediction is that students who are asked to do only a reasonable amount of grammar learning will develop more interest in it. Many will be interested in consciously learning what they have already subconsciously acquired; in other words, they will develop an interest in the structure of language. Thus, the foreign language teacher will eventually be able to teach even more grammar, but in a way that is consistent with the theory (for the Monitor and as sheltered subject matter).

The difficulty of teaching classical literature can be greatly reduced if students have greater competence in the language, if students have done a great deal of lighter reading in the foreign language, and if students have learned to appreciate less daunting texts than those usually presented in literature classes. Consistent with this view are findings that foreign language literature students who had done more leisure reading in the foreign language had the most positive attitudes about literature (Davis, Gorell, Kline and Hsieh, 1992). Thus, the point of view presented here is in no way antithetical to the teaching of classical literature: it facilitates it.

The role of the FL teacher is now expanded, but in ways that are, I believe, interesting. The FL teacher should be familiar with the everyday literature and media of the countries in which the target language is spoken, and be able to help students find books and tapes that interest them. In addition, the FL teacher should know something about language acquisition theory, in order to teach it as part of orientation and as sheltered subject matter. Such knowledge will facilitate the development of efficient strategies that will help students while they are in the program, and after they complete it.

References

Appleby, B. and Conner, J. 1965. Well, what did you think of it? *English Journal* 54: 606-612.

Asher, J. 1994. *Learning Another Language Through Actions: The Complete Teacher's Guidebook.* Los Gatos, California: Sky Oaks Productions.

Bader, L., Veatch, J., and Eldrige, J. 1987. Trade books or basal readers? *Reading Improvement* 24: 62-67.

Beebe, L. 1985. Input: Choosing the right stuff. S. Gass and C. Madden eds. *Input in Second Language Acquisition.* New York: Newbury House.

Cho, K.S. and Krashen, S. 1993. Acquisition of vocabulary from the Sweet Valley High Kids series: Adult ESL acquisition. *Journal of Reading* 37: 662-667.

———. 1995a. From Sweet Valley Kids to Harlequins in one year. *Calfiornia English* 1,1: 18-19.

———. 1995b. Becoming a dragon: Progress in English as a second language though narrow free voluntary reading. *California Reader* 29: 9-10.

Cummins, J. 1991. Interdepence of first- and second-language proficiency in bilingual children. In *Language Processing in Bilingual Children*, E. Bialystok ed. Cambridge, England: Cambridge University Press.

Davis, J., L. Gorell, Kline, R. and Hsieh, G. 1992. Readers and foreign languages: A survey of undergraduate attitudes toward the study of literature. *Modern Language Journal* 76: 320-322.

Dupuy, B. Lecture-cadeau, lecture-plaisir: Des étudiants en FLE se prononcent sur les bénéfices dérivés de la lecture libre. Forthcoming (a).

Dupuy, B. Cercles de lecture: Une autre approche de la lecture dans la classe intermédiaire de français langue étrangère. Forthcoming (b).

Dupuy, B. and McQuillan, J. Handcrafted books: Killing two birds with one stone. In G. Jacobs ed., *Extensive Reading*. In press.

Dupuy, B. and Krashen, S. From lower-division to upper-division foreign language classes: Obstacles to reaching the promised land. *ITL:Review of Applied Linguistics*.In press.

Edwards, H., Krashen, S., Wesche, M., Clement, R., and Krudinier, B. 1985. Second language acquisition through subject-matter learning: A study of sheltered psychology classes at the University of Ottawa. *Canadian Modern Language Review* 41: 268-282.

Elley, W. 1993. Acquiring literacy in a second language: The effects of book-based programs. *Language Learning* 41: 375-411.

Elley, W. and Mangubhai, F. 1983. The impact of reading on second language learning. *Reading Research Quarterly* 19: 53-67.

Graman, T. 1987. The gap between lower- and upper-division Spanish courses: A barrier to coming up through the ranks. *Hispania* 70: 929-935.

Hafiz, F. and Tudor, I. 1989. Extensive reading and the development of language skills. *ELT Journal* 43: 4-11.

Hammond, R. 1988. Accuracy versus communicative competency: The acquisition of grammar in the second language classroom. *Hispania* 71: 408-417.

Ho, K. 1982. Effect of language of instruction on physics achievement. *Journal of Research in Science Teaching* 19: 761-67.

Krashen, S. 1982. *Principles and Practice in Second Language Acquisition.* Hemel Hempstead, UK: Prentice Hall International.

——. 1985. *The Input Hypothesis.* Beverly Hills, California: Laredo Publishing Company, 1985.

——. 1991. Sheltered subject matter teaching. *Cross Currents*, 18: 183-189.

——. 1992. Under what conditions, if any, should formal grammar instruction take place? *TESOL Quarterly* 26: 409-411.

——. 1993a. The effect of formal grammar teaching: Still peripheral. *TESOL Quarterly* 27: 722-725.

——. 1993b. *The Power of Reading*. Englewood, Colorado: Libraries Unlimited.

——. 1994a. The input hypothesis and its rivals. In N. Ellis (ed.) *Implicit and Explicit Learning of Languages*. London: Academic Press. pp. 45-77.

——. 1994b. The pleasure hypothesis. In J. Alatis (ed.) *Georgetown Round Table on Languages and Linguistics*. Washington, DC: Georgetown University Press. pp. 299-322.

——. 1996. The case for narrow listening. *System* 24: 97-100.

Krashen, S. and Terrell, T. 1983. *The Natural Approach: Language Acquisition in the Classroom*. Hemel Hempstead, UK: Prentice Hall International.

Krashen, S. and Kiss, N. 1996. Notes on a polyglot: Kato Lomb. *System* 24: 207-210.

LaBrant, L. 1938. An evaluation of free reading. *In Research in the Three R's*. C. Hunnicutt and W. Iverson eds. New York: Harper and Brothers. pp. 154-161.

Lafayette, R. and Buscaglia, M. 1985. Students learn language via a civilization course - a comparison of second language classroom environments. *Studies in Second Language Acquisition* 7: 323-42.

Lamme, L. 1976. Are reading habits and abilities related? *The Reading Teacher* 10: 21-27.

Lomb, K. 1970. *Igy Tanulok Nyelveket (This is How I Learn Languages)*. Budapest: Gondolat.

Mason, B. and Krashen, S. 1997. Extensive reading in English as a foreign language. *System* 25, 1.

McQuillan, J. 1994. Reading versus grammar: What students think is pleasurable for language acquisition. *Applied Language Learning* 5: 95-100.

Nagy, W., Herman, P., and Anderson, R. 1985. Learning words from context. Reading *Research Quarterly* 17: 233-255.

Nicola, N. 1989. Experimenting with the new methods in Arabic. *Dialog on Language Instruction* 6: 61-71.

Nikolov, M. 1995. *Perspectives on Child Second Language Acquisition in the Classroom*. Doctoral Dissertation, Pécs, Hungary, Janus Pannonius University.

Rucker, B. 1982. Magazines and reading skills: Two controlled field experiments. *Journalism Quarterly* 59: 28-33.

Smith, F. 1988. *Joining the Literacy Club*. Portsmouth, NH: Heinemann Publishing Company.

Smith, F. 1995. *Understanding Reading*. Hillsdale, NJ: Erlbaum.

Southgate, V., Arnold, H., and Johnson, S. 1981. *Extending Beginning Reading*. London: Heinemann Educational Books.

Sternfeld, S. 1992. An experiment in foreign language education: The University of Utah's immersion/multiliteracy program. In R. Courchene, J. Glidden, and J. St. John eds. *Comprehension-Based Language Teaching*. Ottawa: University of Ottawa Press. pp. 407-432.

Swaffer, J. and Woodruff, M. 1978. Language for comprehension: Focus on reading. *Modern Language Journal* 6: 27-32.

Trelease, J. 1995. *The Read-Aloud Handbook*. New York: Penguin. 4th edition.

Wolfe, D. and Jones, G. 1982. Integrating total physical response strategy in a level 1 Spanish class. *Foreign Language Annals* 14: 273-80.